IMAGES
of England

BILLINGSHURST AND WISBOROUGH GREEN

Champion's Smock Mill, Wisborough Green, c. 1909, when it was in the last years of its working life. The mill was built around 1820 and was converted into a dwelling in 1960.

IMAGES
of England

BILLINGSHURST AND WISBOROUGH GREEN

Wendy Lines

TEMPUS

First published 2002
Copyright © Wendy Lines, 2002

Tempus Publishing Limited
The Mill, Brimscombe Port,
Stroud, Gloucestershire, GL5 2QG

ISBN 0 7524 2482 3

Typesetting and origination by
Tempus Publishing Limited
Printed in Great Britain by
Midway Colour Print, Wiltshire

For my daughters Jenna and Linda who are Sussex born and Billingshurst bred.

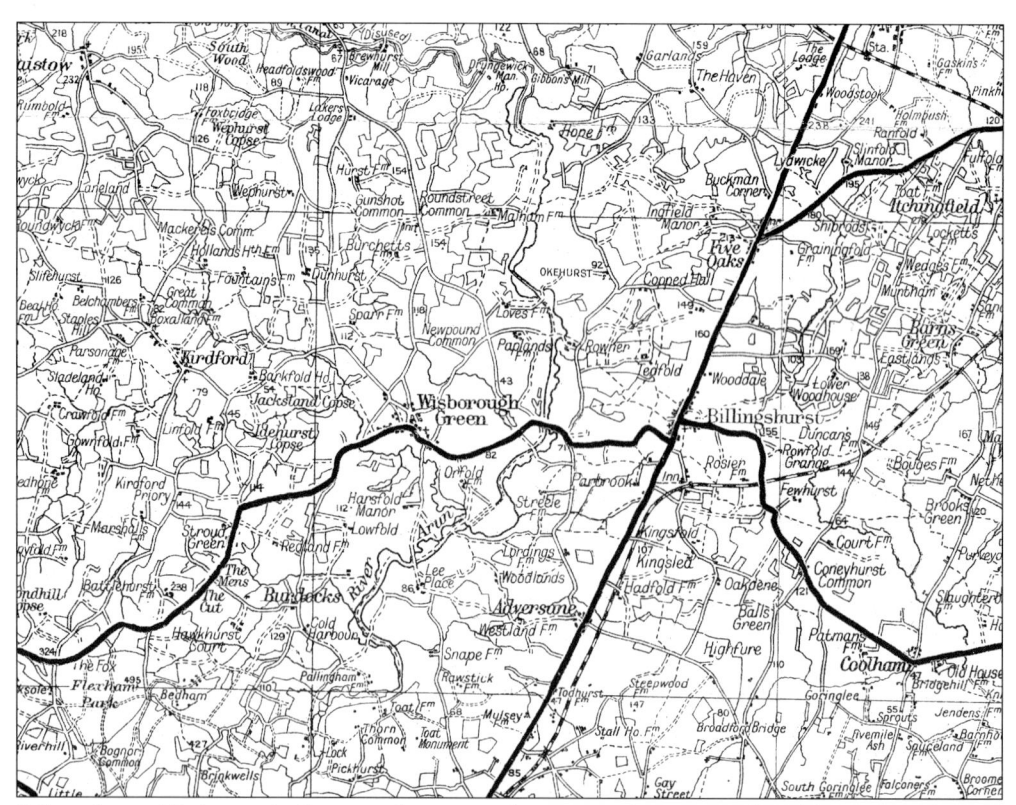

Billingshurst, Wisborough Green and environs from part of a map produced for an estate agent in the 1950s which was based on an Ordnance Survey map.

Contents

Acknowledgements 6

Introduction 7

1. Billingshurst – The Village, the Station Area and the Hamlets 9

2. Wisborough Green – The Village and The Green 59

3. Agriculture 89

4. Schools, Societies and Sports 101

5. The Two World Wars 121

Newbridge in 1909, which spans the River Arun and forms part of the boundary between Billingshurst and Wisborough Green.

Acknowledgements

Warm thanks are due to the people who so generously loaned me photographs and for the enjoyment of the time spent looking at them together. I am also grateful to everyone who named people in the photographs and who helped with local and historical details. They are Dorothy Ayre, Iris Ayre, Barry and Jean Baker, Lena Balchin, Mary and Trevor Benson, Ron and Wendy Boniface, Jean and Henry Botting, Susan Burst, Dick Carter, Myrtle Clark, Sheila Clark, Joyce Dalmon, Rhonwyn Daniel, Daphne Drabble, Betty Eggleden, Don Everson, John Dendy and Susie Evershed, John Farmer, Janet and Robin Francis, Doris Garton, George Goodchild, Radolt Hugely, Marie Hughes, Irene and John Humphreys, Diana Hunnisett, John Hurd, Nancy Kernutt, Matti Kingston, Malcolm Laker, Roger Lugg, Eileen Lund, Roger Lusted, Joy Mann, Sidney Matthews, Ted Merrikin, Peter Newman, Ronnie Oulds, Mrs E. Parker, the Patterson family, Margaret Pegley, Philip Polwin, the late Mrs Dorothy Pullen, Tony Puttick, Alan Redman, Alma Reynolds, Cecil Rhodes, Mr B. Roberts, Cyril Roffe, Mrs J. Russell, Mrs P. Sherlock, Bill and Evelyn Skinner, Deborah Stevenson, Jane Terry, Lindsey Voice, Joan and Charlie West, Jane White, Dr J. Wild and Yvonne Wolczak. Sincere thanks as well go to Billingshurst Dramatic Society, Billingshurst Local History Society, Billingshurst Women's Institute, Ingfield Manor School, The Frank Patterson Appreciation Society, *The Soldier Magazine*, The Trustees of the Women's Hall, *West Sussex County Times*, West Sussex Library Service, *West Sussex Gazette* and the Wisborough Green Trust.

I am grateful to the people who tracked down elusive photographs and who gave advice. They are John Day, Ina Holland, Jenna Lines, Peter Lines, Albert Napper, Chris Rainer, Duncan Reynolds and Gordon Simkin.

I express my appreciation of Billingshurst, Chichester, Horsham and Worthing libraries as well as Horsham Museum and the West Sussex Record Office, for their research facilities.

Many thanks also go to Janet Austin who checked an early draft and to Linda Lines for later corrections of the text.

I have as far as possible checked the authenticity of the material and I apologize to anyone whose copyright I may have inadvertently breached.

Introduction
A Comparison of the Parishes

Billingshurst and Wisborough Green are two adjacent Sussex Wealden parishes. Both were once of similar size. Both places are first mentioned in documents at the beginning of the 1200s, although the settlements probably started in Saxon times.

Farming was the main occupation of most of the inhabitants for centuries but in the late 1500s Wisborough Green was the centre of the local glass industry, while Billingshurst was only on the fringe of it. Wisborough Green also had an iron industry site at Pallingham while Billingshurst had none.

At the beginning of the twenty-first century there are working farms in both parishes, but many surviving timber-framed buildings, situated on ancient landholdings, have been turned into desirable dwellings with little connection to the farming community. However because of the changes in agriculture not so many farmhouses and barns are needed and conversions do preserve the period buildings.

Both parishes have ancient churches with broach spires, situated in a prominent position near the centre of the village settlement. Both churches were restored in the 1860s. Both villages have non-conformists chapels that continue to be used to the present day. Billingshurst has a Roman Catholic church and a United Reformed church, formerly the Congregational church. Wisborough Green had a short-lived Congregational chapel.

Loxwood, a hamlet situated within the parish of Wisborough Green, had its own chapel of St John the Baptist from the early fifteenth century.

In the nineteenth century Loxwood was made into an ecclesiastical parish, and in 1934 the civil parish of Loxwood was formed; thus nearly halving the size of Wisborough Green parish and also its population. A number of the larger houses were situated in the Loxwood end of the parish.

In contrast, Billingshurst had been ceded land to the southwest of its previous boundary up to the banks of the River Arun, which had formerly been part of Pulborough parish.

Wisborough Green is in the Chichester district. The population in 1901 was 1,585; 1,751 in 1931, 980 in 1951 and by 1981 had risen to 1,303.

In the mid-nineteenth century the Wey and Arun canal had considerable influence on the parishes, but this aspect of parish history is well covered by other publications.

There are records of both parishes having small schools in the eighteenth century. Wisborough Green School was built by public subscription in 1852. Billingshurst School was erected in 1865 and was paid for by Mr Carnsew of Summers Place. Both parishes had new primary schools built in the 1970s and the old school premises have been converted into houses. The Weald School for secondary education has been situated in Billingshurst since 1956.

Since the 1950s, Billingshurst has grown to small town size, although it still has a parish council. The north to south bypass was at last completed in 1999, after a wait of fifty years and consequently more houses are being built. The Roman Road of Stane Street, the A29, bisects the parish and the A272 goes east to west and carries on to pass through Wisborough Green. There is a railway station from which many people who live in Billingshurst and the surrounding villages commute to towns mainly to the north of the parish and to London. The several industrial estates in the vicinity of the station also employ people who reside beyond Billingshurst.

Billingshurst is a thriving working community. The village centre has a small supermarket and a varied number of shops. In contrast, Wisborough Green is the quintessential English village with picturesque houses clustered around a large village green. Wisborough Green has never had a railway station and has fewer shops than previously but far fewer new housing developments than Billingshurst. Newpound, formerly the site of the Reliance Works owned by Carter Bros., remains the industrial area of the parish.

Both communities have sporting traditions; the Wisborough Green Cricket Club has always been strong and celebrity matches are played on the green. Wisborough Green Flower Show still takes place in a marquee and attracts a large crowd and the sideshow committee ensures there are plenty of other attractions.

Very few illustrations in the book pre-date the introduction of the picture postcard, which was at the height of its popularity during the Edwardian era (1901-10). The Billingshurst pictures relate more to the whole parish while those of Wisborough Green are mainly concentrated around the vicinity of the village green.

Billingshurst is in the Horsham District. The population in 1901 was 1,591; 2,028 in 1931; 2,955 in 1951 and 5,425 in 1981.

One
Billingshurst – The Village, the Station Area and the Hamlets

The parish church viewed from Carpenters Field, when the churchyard still had room for more burials. The church is the only Grade I Listed building in the parish. Pevsner said, 'The west tower is the best part, dour even in the context of Sussex steeples'. The Women's Hall is partly obscured by a tree to the left but the Caretaker's cottage of the Women's Hall can clearly be seen. At that time the cottage had a larger garden where the washing is seen hanging. A bungalow was later built on this plot. At present the coach station site, in the left middle foreground, is being redeveloped.

The east side of Stane Street showing Hillview Garage when it was decorated for the Coronation of George VI in 1937.

View from the air of Hillview Garage. The image also shows the site of the present junior school, and the corner of the field where Carpenters estate now stands.

Divided-back postcards were first permitted to be used in Great Britain from 1902. Before this, the address had to be written on one side of the card while the message was written on the other side beneath a small picture. A member of the Evershed family was using this old type of card in 1903. The pond referred to in the message would have been near No. 1 Carpenters.

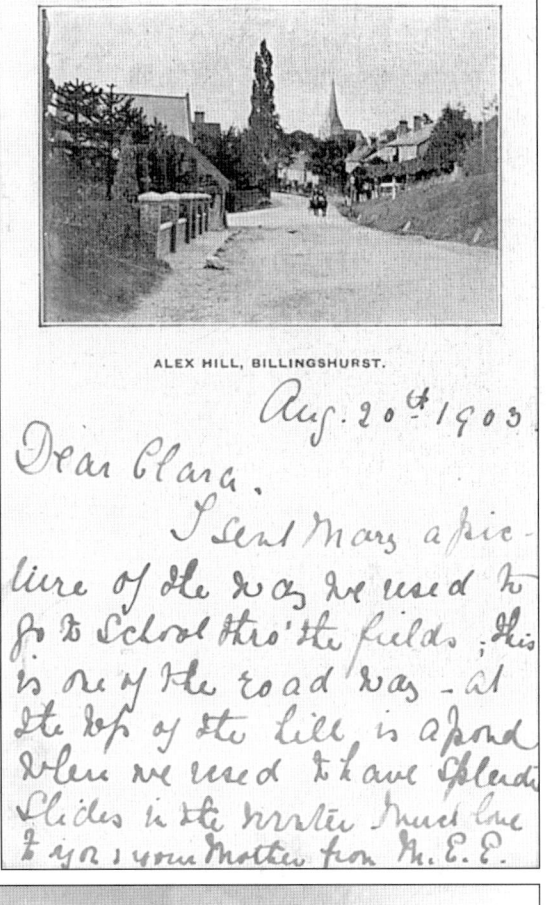

ALEX HILL, BILLINGSHURST.

Aug. 20th 1903

Dear Clara,

I sent Mary a picture of the way we used to go to School thro' the fields; this is one of the road way - at the top of the hill is a pond where we used to have splendid slides in the winter. Much love to you & your Mother from M.E.E.

A rare winter aspect of Alex/ Alecs/ Alicks Hill in the snow, possibly taken during the harsh winter of 1947.

11

West Cott, West Street. The third of three similar cottages situated at the beginning of West Street. The peg tiling has been removed from its front façade.

West Street, c. 1938, showing bungalows now demolished and replaced by houses. Part of West Cott is behind the tree in the left foreground.

The oddly named Bank of England, which used to stand on the opposite side of West Street from the bungalows.

Members of the Congregational church all set for an outing in a Southern Motor Services Ltd, Charabanc, c. 1925. F.A. Skinner, who was a farmer at Cedars, has his elbow over the side of the coach. The group includes the Revd Larkin, Mrs Denman and members of the Radbourne family.

Opening of the new fire station in West Street in 1953. From left to right, back row: Peter Vardy, Arthur Smith, Ted Denman, Tom Topper, Bill Wright, T. Ripley, P. Bryant, Les Banner, Ted Pullen, Chris Davey, J. Giles, Fred Shaw. Middle row: Reginald Playden, Leading Fireman Bernard Matthews, Leading Fireman Dick Slipper, Station Commander Cecil Rhodes, Ernie Grinstead, Fred Denman, George Maybee. Front row: Tom Walker, Jack White, Tizza Longley, Percy Garman.

The National Fire Service first set up village fire brigades in 1938. Brigade members had to work locally. During the Second World War, the Billingshurst Fire Brigade was very active. At first a large Buick saloon was used to pull a trailer pump. A Dennis pump which was housed in a Nissen hut in Jengers Mead replaced this. In 1948 the brigade was taken over by West Sussex Fire Brigade and the new station was completed in 1952/3. While the National Fire Service ran the station it was station No. 32, but after the West Sussex Fire Brigade took over it became station No. 13, because other stations were reluctant to take the No. 13.

The Congregational church built in 1868. It became the United Reformed Church in 1972. Stane Street looks deserted in this postcard dated 1916.

Chapel Corner; all the Victorian and Edwardian houses survive little changed today. In 1911 the partly visible white house, now 95 High Street, was a bakers run by Jabez James Peay. The building was used as a baker's shop for many years, later becoming Cooter's.

South Street, which has been part of the High Street since the 1950s, seen in Edwardian times. The entrance to the Unitarian chapel and 102 High Street is on the left behind the children, one of whom is in an invalid carriage.

The flowering Cherry trees now sadly depleted; this was the picture on the front of Billingshurst Flower Show Schedule in 1969.

The Unitarian chapel/church in the 1930s, formerly the Free Christian church. The chapel/church was originally the General Baptist chapel, and was built in 1754. Inside there is a wall tablet which bears the foundation date and the initials of its two founders, William Evershed and William Turner.

My husband Peter Lines and Shirley Batt in the garden of 2 Arundale Cottages, South Street, now 100 High Street in the mid 1940s, when they were next-door neighbours. The Batt family came to the village from London during the Second World War and stayed in the area. The roof of the Unitarian chapel/church can be seen in the background.

Miss Edith Beck. The photographs of the Beck sisters still grace the walls of the Women's Hall, which they had built for the women of the village in 1923. This was only one example of their generosity towards the village.

Old people in Women's Hall. Mrs Quick is first on the left, and the much loved Nurse Baines third on the right. The photograph of Edith Beck can be seen on the left of this photograph.

Miss Ellen Beck, in the garden of her home Duncans Farm.

Billingshurst Minors' Football Club Dinner in the Women's Hall in the 1950s. The group includes Danny Cherriman, Peter Keyte, Pat and Mr Ede, Betty Burchell, Daphne and Sheila Grinstead, Mrs McGrath, Arthur Smith, Mrs and Mr Hollebone, Arthur Battle, Mrs White, Pat Hollebone, Dennis and Mrs Cox and Mrs Buck.

The parade in South Street in 1911 to celebrate the Coronation of King George V and Queen Mary. Mrs Buskin who wrote a booklet about the event said of the first float 'And now all our loyalty was stirred by the sight of a decorated wagon, one mass of flowers and green containing the well-known figure of Britannia (Miss Laker) wearing a purple robe and glittering helmet. She was supported by Neptune, God of the Waters, (Mr Laker) wearing a grey beard. He was appropriately attired in a dark velvet mantle bordered with ermine and wore a crown. In his hand was the trident. (2nd Prize)'. Some of the photographers of this much-recorded event can be seen on the flat roof a short distance behind 'Neptune's' head.

The King's Arms and South Street, c. 1909. J.B. Dashwood who wrote *The Thames to the Solent by Canal and Sea* would have agreed with the comment written on the front of this card. Dashwood said in 1868 'We found Billingshurst a charming little place with a neat inn The King's Arms; and having secured our rooms and changed our attire, we had the gratification of sitting down to as good a dinner as, I believe, it is possible to get in a quiet country village.'

The King's Arms in the 1920s. Dashwood continued to say about his dinner, 'Everything was fresh and good of its kind; eggs, butter, bread, fruit, cream, all excellent; and mutton-chops done to a turn, with excellent beer and very fair sherry.'

Ye Olde Six Bells when it was a beer house run by Stephen Garman, *c.* 1907. Vegetables were being grown in the front garden.

YE OLDE SIX BELLS
(BUILT AS FARMHOUSE A.D. 1320)

BILLINGSHURST

Sussex.   **Phone Bill. 124**

Fully Licensed.   Residential.

Situated in delightful Countryside half-mile from Station.

Bedrooms fitted with Electric Fires and Bedside Lamps, two with H & C.

Particular attention paid to the Cooking. Own Poultry, etc.

Easy reach of Coast
    Worthing 18 miles,
    Brighton 25 ,,
    Bognor 22 ,,
    London 42 ,,

TARIFF.

Terms include early Tea, Baths and Coffee after Meals.

Bed & Breakfast   15/- per person
Per Week   7½ guineas   ,,   ,,
Per Day   25/-   ,,   ,,

Weekend, from Saturday Tea to Monday Breakfast inclusive, 55/- per person.

Special terms for Easter, Whitsun, August and Christmas.

Under personal supervision,
H. TEMPLE-JONES.

Terms subject to alteration without notice.

Printed and Published by F. Frith & Co Ltd., Reigate

Advertisement for Ye Olde Six Bells produced for Mr Temple-Jones, landlord in the 1950s.

Mill Lane, taken from what is now the library car park. The poplar trees and the building in the right foreground have long since disappeared. This postcard, dated 1906, was sent to Paris but it has returned to Billingshurst!

Frank Patterson's line drawing of Mill Lane, which was published in *Cycling Magazine* in 1920.

This evocative scene shows Mr Linfield haymaking on the remainder of the village green. In the background to the right of the church spire are Causeway and Tithe cottages, which together were once a Wealden house, built in around 1475.

The Causeway and part of the green. The corner shop was then run by W.J. Barnes.

Jack and Leslie Barnes standing outside their father's shop in October 1926. On the extreme right outside the living quarters an advertisement for Brocks Fireworks can be seen.

W. J. BARNES,

Greengrocer & Fruiterer, Confectioner & Tobacconist.

Opposite Post Office, BILLINGSHURST.

ALSO A GOOD SELECTION OF
TOYS, GAMES, BOOKS,
FANCY GOODS, Etc.

An advertisement for W.J. Barnes from *The Billingshurst News*, in the 1920s.

The High Street, c. 1906, showing Laker's Tea Rooms and the barn beside it, which was replaced with the bank buildings, now a solicitor's office. The top of the barn is just visible in the Mill Lane view. The old post office is beyond and most of the present supermarket site is yet to be built on. The ivy covered Brick House can be seen on the right.

A busier-looking High Street in 1948. The proprietors of the lock-up shops on the right included: G. Freeman, C. Trevelyan and A.J. Voice.

The High Street in the 1940s. The first shop on the left then sold luggage and gentlemen's clothes and is now Books and Things. Next door was the International Stores. R.S. Higgins was in the double shop of the former Carlton House. The shop blinds were characteristic of the period.

The High Street, c. 1930. The cottages in the foreground are timber-framed beneath their brick façade, now 44 High Street and the Monsoon Indian Restaurant. Beyond The King's Head, Delaney's Garage was run from part of the malt-house buildings.

George Ware drapers shop, now the funeral directors, is on the immediate right of this post-war card. The shops and houses on this side of the High Street are little different today, but most of the buildings on the left have been demolished. The malt-house buildings already looked in a sorry state.

The Kiln at
"THE MALTINGS"
Luncheon & Tea House
BILLINGSHURST, SUSSEX

Inside the conical tower of The Maltings in the 1930s, long after it had ceased to be used to convert barley into malt for brewing. During the 1930s the premises were used as a hotel and a luncheon and tea house.

The back of the medieval Gingers House, which was part of the Maltings buildings, when they were being demolished. The cone of the malt-house had already been taken down by this time.

The upper-end of the High Street looking south, c. 1904. The Rising Sun public house – later Ivy Cottage – together with Jengers House, behind the sign, and The Maltings have all been demolished. On the left, 13 High Street is little altered and the singled storied building alongside it was soon to be dismantled to make way for the Old Village Hall erected in 1906.

All the houses in the foreground have changed little since 1923, but the front gardens on the right now have a more open appearance. The old Village Hall can be seen centre left. This has been converted into flats.

The upper-end of the High Street in the late 1930s, before Coombe Hill had an opening onto it. April Cottage, Bradgate Cottage and the White House, in the foreground, look nearly the same in 2002.

The filling station owned by the Laker family. The banner advertises Castrol oils. Whitehall House in the background was situated immediately to the south of Roman Way. The house in the foreground is still there and the occupants used to have to pay the Laker family a peppercorn rent of three farthings per annum for the pillar with the white top on the corner of the property. The pillar is still there but Laker's buildings have long since gone!

Bernard Baker the outfitters can be seen on the right in the 1930s, before the windows were enlarged. This is now the site of Lloyds Bank. The building adjoining the premises is Swan House. The single-storied shop was Lusted & Son, in the foreground was R. Crisp, at present Choices. Crisp started as a tobacconist and hairdresser and later sold electrical goods.

31

Smiling Billingshurst residents, who looked happy to queue outside Bernard Baker's shop before a sale in the spring of 1949. The group includes: Mrs Denman, Mrs Hannerford, Mrs Adams, Mrs Claydon, Mrs Elliott, Myrtle Wells/Clark, Mrs Topper, Mrs Grover, Mrs Lugg, Mrs Patterson, Mrs White and her daughter Sylvia.

A Box of Bon-bons lasts for Five Minutes.
A Box of Chocolates, Half an Hour.
A Box of Cigarettes, One Day.
A Bottle of Whiskey---er---well!

But if you give Your Friends Something they can Use They will think of You every Day!

A FEW SUGGESTIONS:

AFTERNOON CLOTHS. BED JACKETS. BRACES. CARDIGANS. CUSHION COVERS. DUCHESSE SETS. DINNER CLOTHS. GLOVES. HAND-BAGS. HATS AND CAPS. HANDKERCHIEFS. HANDKERHIEF SACHETS. JUMPERS. LEGGINGS. MATINEE COATS. MACINTOSHES. NIGHTDRESS SACHETS. OVERALLS. PULLOVERS. PYJAMAS. PYJAMA CASES. PURSES. RUNNERS SOCKS. STOCKINGS. SCARVES. SLIPPERS. SHOES. SHIRTS SLIPOVERS. TIES. TEA CLOTHS. TEA COSIES. TABLE CENTRES. UMBRELLAS. UNDERWEAR. WELLINGTONS. ETC. ETC.

There is a gift in our Store for everyone you know—young or old. Just put on your thinking cap—or better still, come and have a look round.

And don't forget—there will still be a good selection at five minutes to nine on Christmas Eve—BECAUSE we always carry a large stock.

BERNARD BAKER,
BILLINGSHURST AND PULBOROUGH.
Phone 123.   Phone 152.

A Christmas advertisement from *The Billingshurst News*. Bernard Baker wrote all his entertaining advertisements personally. *The Billingshurst News* was a free newspaper which was edited by Charles Tiller from 1929-39.

The Floral Parade held in 1910. In the background is part of Voices monumental yard, where Choices is now situated, and the one-storey building.

Mr E. Birchmore stands outside the same premises, which was a bakery and confectioners, which he ran from 1916 until 1928. The shop, 41a High Street, is now Burford Jordan estate agents and Tack-A-Round, and was Lusted & Son in the 1930-50s, and after that, the Co-op.

East Street in the 1920s. The Dance sisters owned the shop past Brick House for many years.

Church Gate when it was a guesthouse and restaurant. Previously the annex had been a grocer's shop.

The parish church of St Mary, taken from the east, in Edwardian times. The outside wall of the chancel was completely rebuilt during the Victorian restoration and the area of the vestry to the right of the tree was newly built in 1866.

The interior of St Mary's church, in the Edwardian era. J.B. Dashwood said in 1868 that 'Billingshurst church is worth a visit.'

Ada and Marjorie Lugg standing outside Gore Cottages in East Street during the late 1920s.

The imposing Gratwicke House, which was pulled down in the 1960s. Gratwicke Close now occupies the site.

Rowfold Grange, showing the south-west façade. James Hall Renton owned this large Victorian mansion, and on his demise his nephew Major-General Renton inherited the estate. The 1903 Billingshurst Flower Show was held in its grounds. Later the Major-General became president of the Horticultural Society. After his death, the estate was split up and sold in 1977 and the Grange was divided into three dwellings. The property is situated off the A272 to the east of the village.

Duncans Farm off West Chiltington Lane, which used to be the home of Ellen and Edith Beck. This card was sent by a member of the Beck family.

Upper Station Road, c. 1904. An early motor-car can be seen in the distance.

Upper Station Road, c. 1915. All the houses in the foreground are almost the same in appearance in 2002. Cricklewood, on the near left, was the home of the artist Henry Charles Fox for many years. Weald Court flats stand on the malt-house site.

A parade in Upper Station Road, probably a Club Day Parade, organized by a Friendly Society. The headquarters were often based at public houses so maybe the parade is heading for the Railway Inn. The band members are not wearing uniforms, but the crowd is well dressed with nearly everybody wearing a hat.

The level crossing gates at the station from Lower Station Road. The man in the apron may be a member of the Voice family who owned the sub-post office and general stores which can be seen on the left.

Number 1 of the four mills was used for grinding when Thomas Keating Ltd made insect powder in the 1920s and '30s. The firm moved to its present site in 1927 from London.

Insect powder being packed in cartons at the factory.

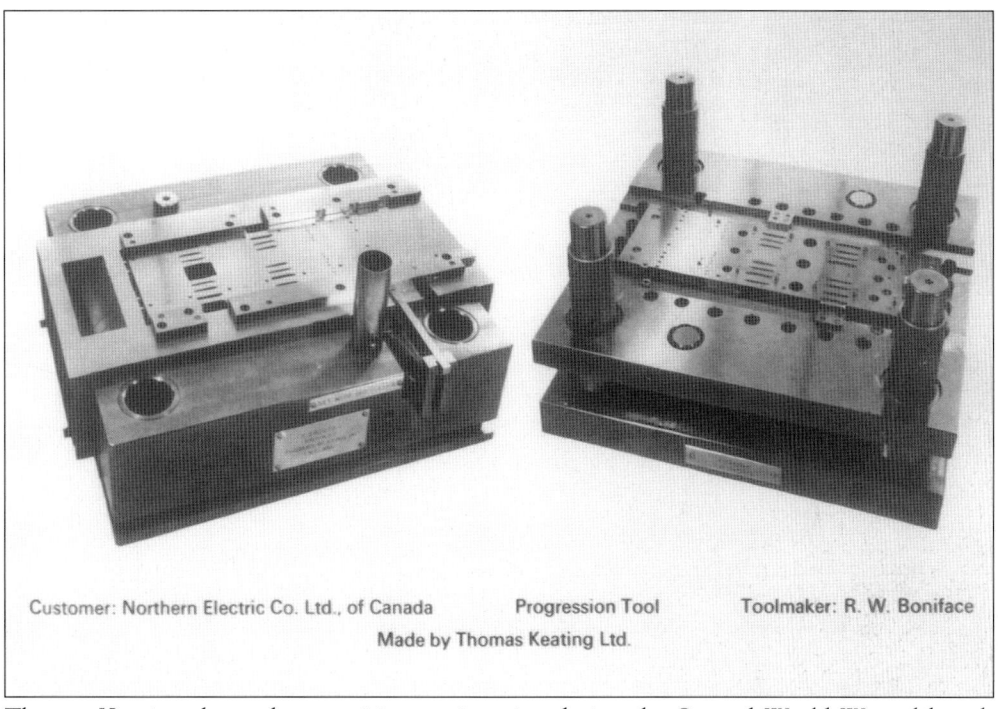

Customer: Northern Electric Co. Ltd., of Canada   Progression Tool   Toolmaker: R. W. Boniface
Made by Thomas Keating Ltd.

Thomas Keating changed to precision engineering during the Second World War, although some insect powder continued to be made until the 1950s.

Precision tools made at Thomas Keating Ltd.

41

Arthur Everson on his motor bike outside Keating's Factory, Daux Road, c. 1930. In the sidecar is his married daughter Winifred and on the pillion his niece Louise. Arthur Everson came from London for a job at Keating's when it opened in Billingshurst. His son also worked there and both generations lived in two of the four houses owned by Keating's in Chestnut Road. Members of the family reside in Billingshurst to the present day.

A very early photograph of wood stacked in the hoop sheds, which were situated near the station and owned by the Puttock family. Wooden hoops that went around barrels were made there from around 1850 to 1950. Great Daux farmhouse is in the background.

Great Daux farmhouse. The right-hand side of this medieval house has close-studded timber framing, the only example of this type of framing to survive in the parish.

Before all the factories were built in Daux Road in the mid-1950s. All the girls worked at Dalam Product Ltd which was termed a paper converters and made cigarette papers and later, Toni perm tissue. From left to right, back row: Mrs Smith, Miss Corby, -?- (bending forward), Betty Eggleden. Front row: Barbara Bristow, -?- , -?- , Rose Morgan.

43

S.C. Reynolds's shop in Lower Station Road during the 1960s. From left to right: Alice Bristow, Len Tetley, a representative from Spar advertising Australian produce, Barbara Terry, Alma and Sidney Reynolds. The premises were until recently a post office and have lately been converted into two take-away restaurants.

S. C. REYNOLDS

JEFFRIES STORES

STATION RD., BILLINGHURST, Sussex

Grocery, Provisions and Greengrocery

A GENUINE DESIRE TO SERVE AND HELP
Cheerful, Courteous Attention to All Enquiries

An advertisement for Reynolds's, 1951.

Opposite in the 1920 and '30s was a general store owned by R. George. The much-altered building is at present a paper and convenience shop.

Richard George's delivery van. Mr. George had two shops. His butcher's shop was at the premises later owned by the Reynolds.

Spring in Lower Station Road during the 1920s. This postcard was produced for W.J. Barnes (see pp. 24 and 25).

Mr Penfold who lived at Five Oaks, delivering milk in Lower Station Road before the First World War.

Beyond Marycot in the foreground can be seen the building which was the Roman Catholic church from 1925 to '61.

The interior of the Roman Catholic church. Although the rest of the building has long since been demolished, the wall with the alcoves on the right can still be seen. It is joined to the outside wall of Marycot, but extends beyond the house.

These houses in Parbrook are little altered, but Stane Street Road looks rough and deserted, c. 1912.

Parbrook in the 1930s. The building premises of Charles Wadey & Sons were in the single storey building, and two cottages occupied the site of its present offices. A barn – since demolished – can be seen through the trees on the right.

Until recently, this timber-framed house was a restaurant called The Gables. Previously it was called Great Grooms, the name currently used by the adjacent Antiques Centre.

Parbrook looking north in the 1950s. This view was taken from approximately where the roundabout of the new bypass is situated.

Beke House. A large timbered building brought from Suffolk in 1926 but which, due to a road-widening scheme, was later dismantled and re-erected in Marringdean Road. In style it was unlike Sussex timber-framed houses. Unfortunately this building was mysteriously gutted by fire in 1967. A swimming pool now occupies part of its site and a modern house has been built nearby.

High Fure, Marringdean Road in 1912. This Edwardian house stands on an ancient landholding which was part of the manor of Ferring and Fure. Ferring being on the Sussex coast and Fure being one of the holdings in a narrow strip of land, situated in Billingshurst directly inland north of Ferring.

Adversane Intermediate Cabin used to be situated on the south-east corner of the level crossing. Part of one of the gates can be seen on the left of the photograph.

Old House at Adversane in the 1960s, which continues to be an Antiques centre and restaurant. Under its brick façade lies a fine timber-framed building and its large medieval timbers can be seen upstairs.

The Malt-house cottages in the 1950s, when Frank Sharville kept a post office and shop in the end cottage. His dog Prince is sitting at the end of the front wall.

Fancy Dress Parade at Adversane, c. 1950. From left to right, back row: Rene ?, Anthony Evershed, Barbara Wickham, Raymond Wickham, Marilyn Balchin, the Klineberg sisters, Shirley Stilwell, Derek Gregory, -?- , -?- . Front row: Deborah Evershed, Julie Humphrey, Thelma Stilwell, Audrey Gregory and Patch, the Gregory's dog. The gamekeeper is holding a dead rabbit!

The Blacksmiths Arms and blacksmith's forge. The latter has been demolished. Gaius Carley's name is above the door; he was the last of a long line of blacksmiths who plied their trade from the site.

The Leconfield hunt at Lordings.

Lordings on the Lordings Road (B1231), still a working farm and the home of the Ayre family.

Lordings during repairs when the timber-framing under the front façade had been exposed. The framing is of a dropped tie-beam construction, to allow for more room for storage in the lofts. Richard Penfold who died in 1673 kept wheat and wool in the lofts.

The Five Oaks public house, c. 1910, with cottages behind it long since demolished.

The Five Oaks Inn, looking more how many people will remember it. In my last book I said that this was a new façade on the old inn, but after seeing this postcard it seems more likely that the pub was completely rebuilt. In turn this building has also been demolished with no replacement, so for the first time in 150 years there is no inn at Five Oaks.

Houses on the A29 approaching Five Oaks from Billingshurst in 1925, the single storied building was for a time a reading room.

Sir Charles Fielding. Knighted for his services to industry, he was also a prominent member of the local community and owned land in both Billingshurst and Wisborough Green.

56

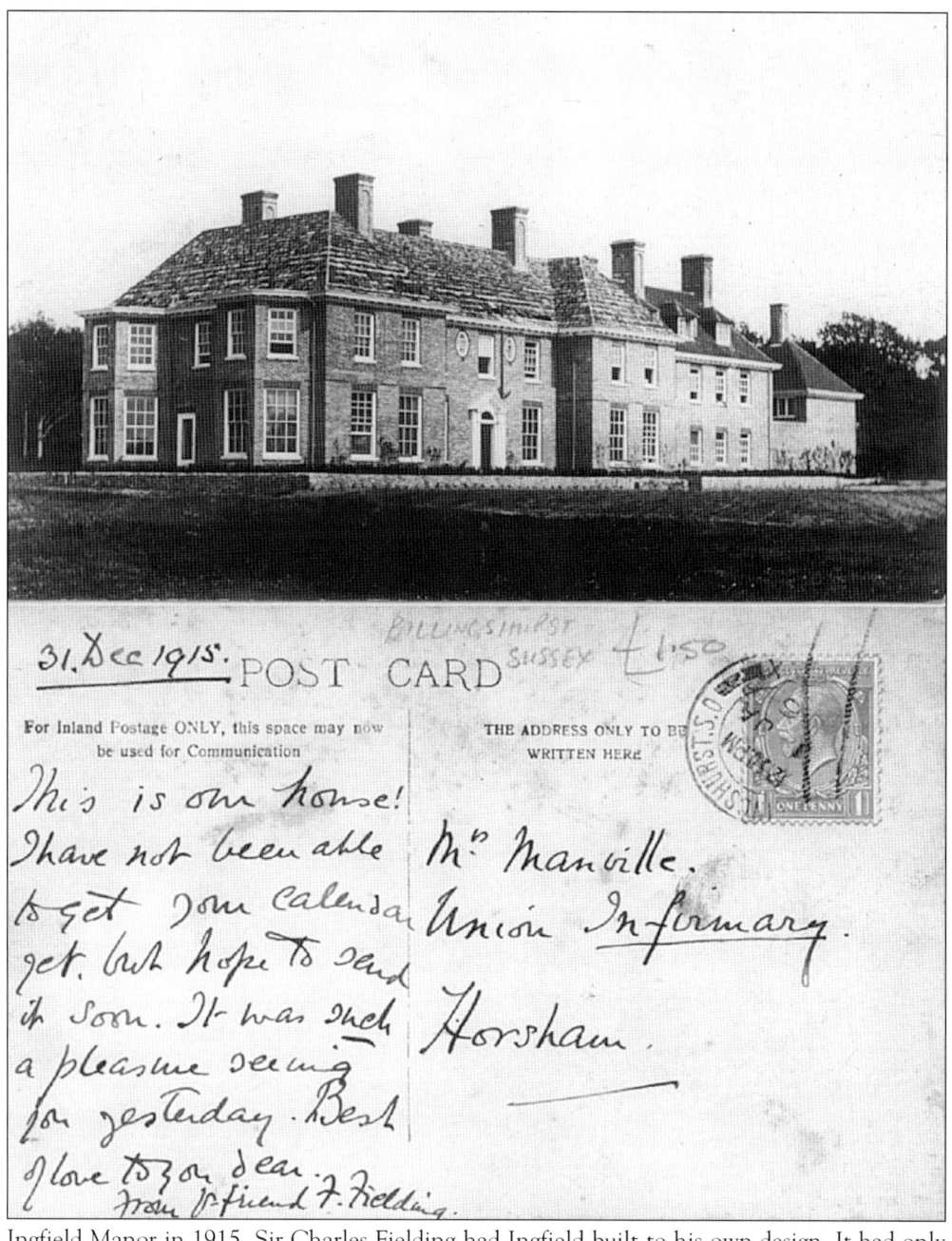

Ingfield Manor in 1915. Sir Charles Fielding had Ingfield built to his own design. It had only been completed a few years when his wife Frances sent this postcard. The site has been used as a school for children with Cerebral Palsy since 1961.

Rowner Mill in the 1930s, which was part of Pulborough parish until the parish boundaries were reorganized in 1934. However, because it was geographically nearer to Billingshurst, Rowner is mentioned in Billingshurst's parish records.

Rowner Mill in the 1960s shortly before it was demolished.

Two
Wisborough Green
The Village and The Green

An Edwardian aspect of the three dominant buildings of the village; the church, workhouse and tithe barn. A copy of a document dated 1635 regarding the glebe/church lands and tithes said 'There belongeth to the Parsonage impropriate a large barn 17 acres of land by estimation all the Tythe of Hay & Corn Hempe Flax growing in the fields and plowed with the plow the Gratten Grass [which we commonly call White hay] being excepted which by the custom of the parish does not pay tithe at all'.

The A272 approaching Wisborough Green from Billingshurst. The barn and shed have been demolished. Farngates cottage which has since been much extended, is to the left of the farm buildings; the Elms is further on the left in the background.

The Parish church from Harsfold Lane. The growth of trees currently obscures the view of the church from the lane, especially in the spring and summer.

Another view further down Harsfold Lane, from near Simmonds Bridge, *c.* 1908. The farm building below the church is now a ruin.

The imposing Harsfold Manor built in 1890, for John Arthur Wyatt, on a hill to the west of the old farmhouse called Harsfold. Mr Wyatt was a much-loved figure in the village. He died whilst out hunting on his favourite mare Marionette. The *Parish Magazine* of June 1925 records a garden fete held at Harsfold Manor, at which five hundred people attended and £90 was raised towards the church-heating fund.

The church of St Peter *Ad Vincula* (in chains) during Edwardian times, when some of the gravestones were in pristine condition. The church shares its unusual dedication with two well-known places, York Minster and the chapel in the Tower of London.

The interior of the church in 1907, when it was lit with hanging oil lamps. The text around the chancel arch is no longer visible. The wall painting was discovered accidentally by workmen during the 1868 restoration and can be seen to the right of the chancel arch. Henry Napper of Laker's Lodge, situated in Loxwood, did the first drawing of the wall painting when it was uncovered.

The Parish church, c. 1905. The church is mainly Norman and early English. It was restored in 1868. The exterior of the spire looks similar, but more slender, to that of St Mary's, but the internal structure is different.

The church and the workhouse. The church was in pre-Reformation times a place of pilgrimage. The church owned a number of relics, which in 1538 had to be surrendered to Sir William Goring by order of King Henry VIII. The fourteen relics included a piece of the hair and beard of St Peter, and St Thomas of Canterbury's vestments. The part of the workhouse in the picture has been demolished and the remainder of the building has been used as the village hall since 1956. The workhouse is said to be built on the site of a Benedictine monastery.

The lower stone-built wing of the workhouse and the end of the larger three-storied brick built cross-wing. In 1835 it was decided 'that the Workhouse at Wisborough Green be appropriated to the reception of children of both sexes and be enlarged and altered as to contain 200 children'. This was after new Poor Law Acts were passed when parishes had to join together to form Unions. Wisborough Green became part of the Petworth Union and so did Billingshurst until 1870, when it became part of the Horsham Union.

Churchgates. Standing to the left is Arthur Mann who was born at the house in 1891. In the picture above, the house had its main door in the front façade.

The Church, Wisborough Green

The barn in front of Churchgates has been converted to a house called Churchgates Barn. Part of the old workhouse can be seen on the right. The low building adjacent to it with the chimney has been demolished and an outside staircase now leads to a flat above the village hall. Thomas Melville was the master and his wife Elizabeth the matron of the workhouse in 1871 when they looked after over thirty children from Wisborough Green and other villages in the Petworth Union.

A Second World War programme. The WI meeting room was situated in the village hall. Wisborough Green had an active branch of the GTC run by Mrs Barlow, and a long tradition of raising money for Dr Barnardo's Homes. From 1920 to the 1950s the remainder of the workhouse was turned into accommodation for four families.

— A —

Variety Show

will be given by

THE WISBOROUGH GREEN
GIRL'S TRAINING CORPS

IN THE W.I. ROOM

on Wednesday, Dec. 5th,

at 7.30 p.m.

in aid of

Dr. Barnardo's Homes

SILVER COLLECTION

Programmes 3d. each, or Donation to the above fund

Doors open at 7.15 p.m.

The village or horse pond in Edwardian times. In both this and the following postcard the place where horses were watered can be seen. The pond was also used for filling steam engines. The corner of the tithe barn can be seen below the windmill.

Another Edwardian aspect of the pond. Did all the children come from Wisborough Green or were they added later to make the card more interesting? Sometimes Edwardian postcard producers did this.

A much later view of the pond. In the background through the trees can be seen Nos.1-2 High Barn, part of which was once a butcher's shop.

Thomas Dennett wearing the regalia of an Oddfellow, stands outside No. 2 High Barn when it was a butcher's shop. The Oddfellows, which still operates today, is a Friendly Society.

67

In the background of this picture is the Three Crowns. The bus shelter is still there today, but opposite, the premises of H. Balchin the builder and the adjacent Handy Shop have both been demolished.

The old post office, now a house called White Chestnuts, and next door Grene Cottage. White Chestnuts was a general store from 1931-72, run by Mr and Mrs James whose son was the proprietor of the Handy Shop. Grene Cottage looks as though the roof structure is of a drop tie-beam construction, similar to Lordings of Billingshurst. Green House abuts Grene Cottage at its back.

The same two houses showing their location in 1905. The pollarded willow tree trunks have quite small diameters. They can be seen in various stages of growth in all the previous images of the pond. The sub-postmistress at this time was Miss Emma Wadey.

W. Tickner's carriers van outside the Three Crowns in the 1880s. Carriers formerly played an important role in village life bringing articles otherwise unobtainable to villages and delivering goods from the villages to other places on their route. William Tickner went to Horsham via Billingshurst on Tuesdays and Saturdays returning the same day, and to Guildford on Thursday returning on Friday.

69

The Three Crowns. The landlord of the public house in 1907 was George Champion, who also owned the windmill. In 1866 the landlady of the Three Crowns was Elizabeth Voice. She must have kept the pub on after the death of her husband John who was listed as the landlord in 1858.

The Three Crowns, workhouse and the church in the Edwardian era. The tithe barn, now converted to a dwelling called Glebe Barn, can be seen by the church. This is a view much favoured by the Edwardian postcard photographers.

A line drawing by Harold Roberts, which was sold as a postcard in 1951. Harold Roberts was an artist who lived in the village. His younger son Luther (1923-88) was a skilful artist as is his elder son Bevil, who continues to reside in Wisborough Green.

'The Hunt at Wisborough Green' also by Harold Roberts.

71

Upfield is seen here in the left foreground and Champions Windmill in 1896, when it was in full working order. The tall shed has long since disappeared, but it was probably connected to the blacksmiths. There are several horses and Mr Carter of Sweephurst Farm says that 'the sail of a daisy reaper' can be seen in the background. (Photograph by courtesy of the West Sussex Library Service, Worthing Library.)

Upfield's Stores and Forge Cottage in Edwardian times. By the mid-nineteenth century the Upfield family had established a grocery and drapers shop in the village. Until Allen Watts Upfield took over the store in the 1870s female members of the family, Sarah and Elizabeth, had run the shop for twenty years.

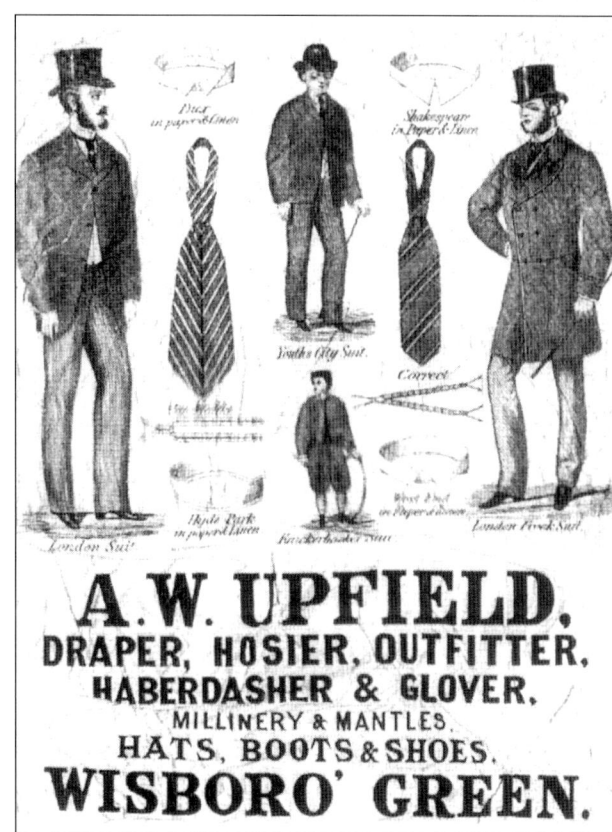

A delightful advertisement for A.W. Upfield in the 1890s, when Allen Watt Upfield was the proprietor.

A.W. UPFIELD,
DRAPER, HOSIER, OUTFITTER,
HABERDASHER & GLOVER,
MILLINERY & MANTLES.
HATS, BOOTS & SHOES.
WISBORO' GREEN.

By the 1920s the shop had become Forest Stores. To the right of the shop stood the blacksmith's buildings. Now called Forest Place, the store building was converted into luxury apartments nine years ago, much to the regret of older residents who wanted it kept as a shop.

May Day on the Green, *c.* 1953. The Forest Stores is on the right. May Day was always a big event at Wisborough Green School. The Carter family presented the maypole to the school.

The Green, Wisborough Green.

A distant panorama of the Green. The paved path which used to traverse the Green can be clearly seen. This was later removed because the paving was considered to be a danger to cricketers. A dispute then ensued about the re-use of the paving.

The house in the foreground is called Farthinghoe, but it was formerly Butts House and is little changed today from 1908, except that the attractive veranda in front of the house has been removed. Fortunately though it survives on one side. Beyond can be seen Butts Cottage and Butts Villa dating from 1896 and standing by itself Ivy Cottage, formerly Recreation Cottage. The same path as in the last postcard can be seen above the lounging boy.

The road through the Green, before the lay-by on the left was installed, The Cricketers Arms can be seen in the distance.

Children from Wisborough Green School celebrating May Day in 1947. The group includes, from left to right; Betty Hook, Joan Hook, June Fielder, Pat Golledge, Jennifer Poat, Hazel Best, June Pullen, Glynis Andrews, Monty Smith, Michael Gent, Peter Brougham.

A view from the Kirdford Road, *c.* 1904. The church and Upfields are in the background and the Green was set up for football. The two ladies look fashionably dressed for such a rural setting.

The cottage called The Luth was a small timber-framed two-up-two-down building at the time the photograph was taken and has since been extended to make it more suitable for modern living.

The picturesque Park Cottage, c. 1907. This was originally timber-framed under its brick and tile façade. An asymmetrical roof-line is often found in older houses. The barn fortunately also survives situated by the Kirdford Road. The Cricketers Arms is in the background.

The Green and, from left to right: The Nook, built in 1900; the house now called Poachers Paddock; The Cricketers Arms and North Cottage.

The Cricketers Arms. Before the premises became a public house it was a beer house for many years.

Brookbridge House, which is situated on Durbans Road. Harvey Piper was sentenced to one months hard labour in 1862 for 'Disgraceful conduct in disturbing a Religious Ceremony' held there. Piper broke the door frame and windows and swore, saying 'Be you a ——— Cokeler?!' The worshippers were indeed Cokelers or members of the Society of Dependants, the sect that is more often associated with Loxwood.

The White House was converted into two dwellings approximately thirty years ago. The block nearest the church is still called The White House. The wing at right angles to the road is now called The Gate House.

Wisborough Green School and the Workhouse, c. 1907. Education was carried on in both institutions. Over sixty children in the workhouse were described as 'scholars' in the 1851 census, when a schoolmistress was employed to educate them.

THE CLOCK HOUSE, WISBOROUGH GREEN, SUSSEX 4

Back to the A272. The timber-framed Clock House, John Streeter who was a clockmaker and mender once lived there. Formerly the building was called Jacklands Farm.

Champions Windmill in 1914. Mr Champion, the last owner, made several unsuccessful attempts to right the displaced windmill cap, which was finally taken off in 1915 by the local builder Mr Balchin.

81

Knights Cottage seen here when it was a butcher's shop run by A.W. Knight; the house was formerly called Whitley Villa. The side of the hairdresser's salon can be seen on the left of the next photograph, but in this one it is yet to be built.

The May Queen and her attendants in Maurice Carter's decorated farm wagon, in 1954. The BBC televised this event for *Children's Newsreel*. From left to right, back row: Pat Wareham, Pamela Medhurst, Jennifer Poat, Rosemary Hook the May Queen, her twin sister Elizabeth, Connie Watson, May Farhall. In front: Kathleen Mitchell, Dorothy Holder.

The Nursing Home, Wisborough Green.

The nursing home is now called Yew Trees and next door Yew Tree Cottage. The timber-framing has been exposed on this house and the front door moved. The nursing home is minus the ivy, but still has the now-trimmed yew trees and both houses still have the railings intact. The house was a nursing home before 1945.

Wickets Cottage is on the left. It is now one house, but was formerly Nos. 1 and 2 Northview. Yew Trees and the timber-framed Yew Tree Cottage, partly obscured by a tree, are beside the present post office and Wisborough Green stores. This was a grocery shop in the early decades of the twentieth century run by Thomas Garrett. Next door is Jasmine Cottage and the last dwelling is Albion House.

Looking along the A272 towards Petworth. Pimpernel House is on the right, across the road Albion House is on the left and beyond are Coed Afal and the roof of Chapel House.

Stanley Kernutt and Nancy Mann outside the Zoar chapel after their marriage in 1951. Nancy's parents, Arthur and Tilly, were caretakers of the chapel and lived in the adjacent Chapel House. The chapel was founded in 1753 and enlarged in 1821. The Calvinistic Methodists were at the chapel in 1874. It now has close links with the Kirdford chapel and is affiliated to the Free Independent Evangelical Churches.

Milland Cottages, which has reverted to being one dwelling. The Mann family lived in one of the cottages before moving to Chapel House.

Matilda 'Tilly' Mann with her daughter Nancy outside Milland Cottages in 1934.

The Goodchild family in the front garden of No. 1 Laurel Cottage in the 1950s. Mary and William Goodchild met and married in India, where their eldest son was born. They settled in Wisborough Green in the 1930s, where a number of their descendants still live. The adults are from left to right, back row: Jim Goodchild, Shirley Smith, who was brought up by the family, Joan, wife of John Goodchild and Irene Goodchild. Second row: Joyce Goodchild and her husband George. Front row: Helen Vicery the Goodchild's only daughter, Mary and William Goodchild.

The Congregational chapel and Laurel Cottages, c. 1927. The chapel was built in 1909, seated 120 people and has since been converted into a house called 'Old Church'. Laurel Cottages are three dwellings and are little changed on the exterior in 2002.

Green Bridge, which spans the Petworth road just outside the village. The brook is sometimes called Green River, but more accurately it is part of the River Kird.

The River Kird, which joins the Arun at Orfold, with Green Bridge in the background.

Wisborough Green, c. 1920.

88

Three
Agriculture

Haymaking at Clevelands, c. 1920. The horses, wagons and ricks recall a bygone era. Mr Linfield is first on the left, behind the white horse, in this carefully posed picture. Clevelands was owned by the Puttock family and is the site of the modern Cleve Way, Billingshurst.

Mr Linfield turning hay at Clevelands in the 1920s.

SCOTCH SEED POTATOES.

MIDLOTHIAN EARLY.	BRITISH QUEEN
DUKE OF YORK.	GREAT SCOT.
SIR J. LLEWELLYN.	MAJESTIC.
EARLY ECLIPSE.	UP-TO-DATE.
SHARPE'S EXPRESS.	FACTOR.
EPICURE.	KERR'S PINK.
KING GEORGE.	ARRAN CHIEF.
ARRAN COMRADE.	KING EDWARD.
ALLY.	THE BARON.

18 Varieties, All One Price.

7 lb. 1/-.   14 lb. 1/10.   28 lb. 3/6.

Special Quotations for Larger Quantities.

F. W. WATT & SONS,
Station Granaries,
BILLINGSHURST.

An advertisement from *The Billingshurst News*, 15 February 1930, regarding the sale of seed potatoes.

The F.W. Watts & Sons Ltd stand at the Horsham Agricultural Show in the 1950s. The firm had a corn merchants business at Hereford House, Station Road, Billingshurst, from 1926-92.

Children picking potatoes at Renvyle, Okehurst Lane in the 1940s. The boy with the bucket is George Longley.

Making a rick with an elevator and horse and two-wheeled cart at Juppsland, Adversane in the 1930s. Robert Ayre Junior is holding the horse and part of an elevator can be seen in the background.

Gordon Lugg steam threshing, on the site of the Weald School, for Dr Puttock of Clevelands in 1940. The Lugg family lived at Gore Farm and James Opie Lugg, Gordon's father, served an apprenticeship at Carter Bros. Steam engines became his speciality and the main business of the family was threshing.

Les Maybee driving a tractor with a rotor baler at Rainbow Field, Bridgewaters, Billingshurst, in 1953.

Christian holidaymakers at Bridgewaters, c. 1953. Behind them is the bale rick they helped to build.

Robert Ayre about to deliver milk from Bridgewaters Farm to the Express Dairy at Billingshurst station, c. 1952.

Marjorie Lugg in 1934 delivering milk for Barnes Dairy, the same family who had the shop on the Causeway, Billingshurst.

Robert Ayre with his son Rob docking Exmoor horn ewes at Five Oaks, in the 1930s.

Dorothy and Ruth Ayre with hand-reared lambs, outside Lordings, *c.* 1937.

Robert Ayre going to market with a calf which is netted in the back of his car, c. 1930. This was taken outside Bridgewaters, approximately where the new bypass is now situated.

Fruit pickers at Howfold Farm, Wisborough Green. Thomas Dennett is fifth from the right.

Part of Carter Brothers stand at the 1905 Horsham Show, although advertised as Carter Bros., Billingshurst, the premises were situated at The Reliance Works, Newpound, Wisborough Green. The four Carter brothers founded the firm of agricultural engineers in 1885.

An early Ferguson tractor in Kent. Sidney Carter is third from right and fourth from right is Frank Williams who was Company Secretary to the Carter Brothers and lived in Billingshurst.

The Carter Bros. stand at one of the Royal Shows, showing Dual-purpose Elevators and a Carter's Ditch Cleaner.

The Reliance oil engine which was made in three sizes by Carter Bros. An engine similar to this attracted the attention of the managing director of Blackstone & Co. Ltd of Stamford, when it was displayed at the Royal Show at Windsor in 1895. Frank and Evershed Carter were persuaded to take their engine to Stamford where Blackstone developed it further.

A 'one-off machine' which was used to roller the putting/bowling green, which was situated outside the Bat and Ball near Carter's Works. It was probably designed by James Carter and had forward and reserve belts and a differential.

A large Elm tree outside Carter's Reliance Works at Newpound. Harry Chivers, who was previously a sailor, is on the right, with Jim Bacon, who used to drive the Garrett tractor that hauled timber.

99

An engine belonging to the Evershed family. One of the three men pictured is Jim Bacon. Unfortunately, the names of the other two are unknown.

James Carter sent this postcard in 1909. The message concerned repairing a binder belonging to a farmer in Surrey. It was probably the same type of binder illustrated on the front of the card.

Four
Schools, Societies and Sports

A successful sports team from Billingshurst School in 1952 at Petworth Park. From left to right, back row: Pam Green, Jean Ayling, Rosalind Birmingham, George Covey, Dr Frank Moreton (headmaster), David Potter, Tony McGrath, Valerie Holmes, Ray Kitchener (?). Third row: Peter Messingham, Lesley Bicknell, Pat Harrison, Rosemary Ahern, Hazel Bicknell, Margaret Grantham, Heather Homer, Jean Napper, Diana Lee (with the cup and she deserves another one for remembering the names of all these people!), Gwennie Birmingham, Rosalind Botting, Violet Keywood, -?-, -?-, Beth Beacher, Hazel Baugh, Hazel Humphrey, Roland Cherriman, Peter Rogers, John Bristow. Second row: Brian Kitchener, Stella Appleton, Danny Reid, Patsy Beadell, Peter Hopkins, Sheila Knight, Wally Cable, Brian Heath, Front row: David Morris, Peter Meadows, Annette Blewett, Dougie Groves, Anne Carr, Roy Elliott, Elizabeth Brooker, Irak Beacher (?), ? Holmes, -?-, Margaret La Roque, Carol Lee, -?- , Brian Pullen, Garfield McFarlane.

Empire Day at Billingshurst Council School in the 1920s, taken in the Infants playground with the 1866 school building in the background. The group includes: P Holdsworth, Jack Topper, Ernie Ayre, Doris Skinner, Joan Pierce, Mable Skinner, Mrs Isted, Jack Gravett, Ron Holdsworth, Fred Stenning, Eric Rice, Peter Woods, Freda Taylor, Hilda Gibson, Blanche Eliott, Doris Pavey, Daisy Stay, Rita and Grace Buckland, Stella Aldridge and Peggy Wood.

Billingshurst Infant School, c. 1931. From left to right, back row: John Martin, Wally Etheridge, Ron Hook, Derek Sims, Keith Cookson, Ted Tiller, Leslie Truelove. Middle row: Edna Bennet, Nora Skinner, Doris Buckland, Eileen Iddington, June Matthews, Archie Hazlewood, Dorothy Elliot, Charlie Penfold. Front row: Doreen Howard, Eileen Humphrey, Marie Everson, Joyce Dalmon, Brian Bushel, Kenneth Bracewell.

Wisborough Green Council School, with staff and pupils. The school was opened in 1852 and extended in 1876 and 1904, when 168 children attended the school.

Wisborough Green School, c. 1908. In the second row, Evelyn Dunkerton is third from the right and her sister Dorothy stands behind her. On the right is Mr Crawford who was the headmaster for thirty-two years. He was also Honorary Secretary to the Flower Show for twenty-five years. One of the boys is his son Victor, who was a great practical joker, but who was unfortunately killed during the First World War.

Wisborough Green School, c. 1912. Annie Dennett is first on the left in the front row and the tallest boy in the back row is Harry Dennett. Mr Crawford is at the back on the right.

Wisborough Green School, c. 1957. A new school was opened in Newpound Lane in 1972.

Maypole dancing in the school playground on what looks like a wet and cold day in the 1960s.

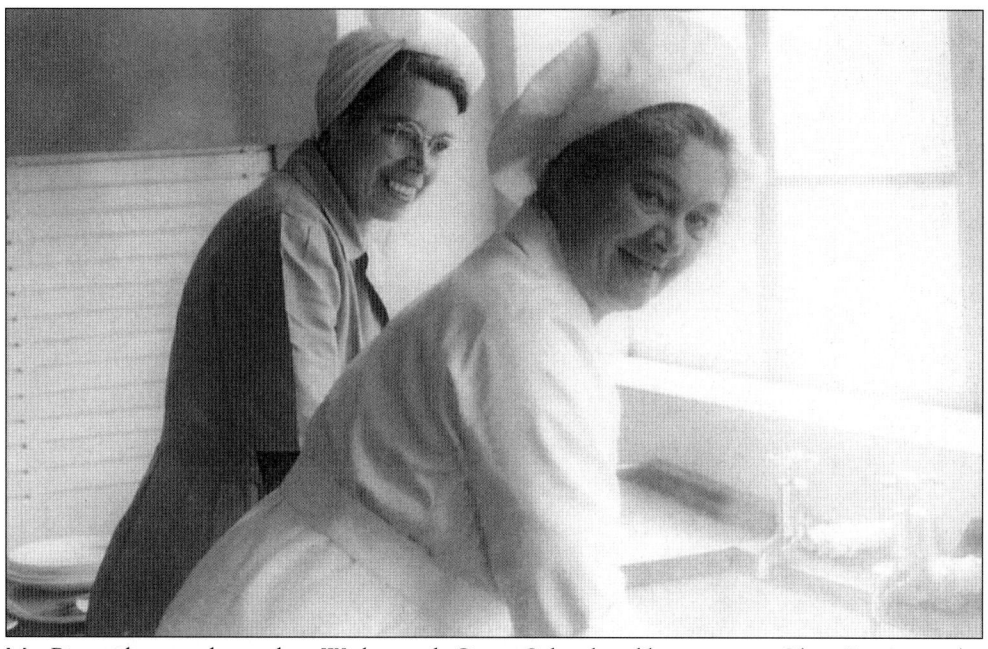

Mrs Pipe, who was the cook at Wisborough Green School and her assistant Olive Stemp, in the days when a cooked school dinner was the norm.

A nativity play at Ingfield Manor School, 1963. Left to right: Anne Tennebaum, Richard Critchley, Julia Dickenson, Elizabeth Fox and Ellen Palmer, and in front, Dianne Selby and Anne Baxter. At this time most of the pupils were boarders. One of the original concepts of the school was that the children slept in the Manor House (see page 57) and went to school in the new classrooms.

Kenneth Baxter and Bronwen Rigby, sitting in the doorway to one of the classrooms at Ingfield in the 1960s. Ken is now married to Elizabeth, one of the 'angels' in the picture above. Some years they drive to Ingfield on its Fete Day to visit and support their old school, which now belongs to Scope, previously the Spastics Society and before that the National Spastics Society.

Tennis courts in the foreground at the Convent of the Immaculate Heart of Mary, Summers Place, Billingshurst. Summers Place was a day and boarding school for girls from 1945-84.

The Kindergarten classroom at the Convent.

A float from the 1911 Coronation Parade, Billingshurst. Mrs Buskin says in her booklet, 'Now an elegant little trap drove up, filled with dainty "maids of Japan" carrying their bright paper umbrellas and looking as if they has stepped out of the "Geisha play"! Their bright sparkling faces gazed forth from a bower of beauty, for the entire vehicle was covered with flowers, and garlands of dark blue blossoms arrested the eye... This was Mrs Alvis' [of Lordings] own trap... an escort of Boy Scouts followed, bearing flags and the Japanese driver lead the cart. (All these children came from Dr Barnado's Home, that splendid institution with "the door that is never shut" for succour is *always given,* even when no money is in the bank. Help is VERY URGENTLY needed to meet the expenses. Should these lines meet the eyes of someone who had both the *heart* and the *means* to help, will he (or she) remember it is Coronation Year, and assist this noble work?).'

No other early photograph of either scouts or guides in the area has yet been found. The Billingshurst Scout Troop was formed in 1910 and the Guides in 1918. The Guides and Scouts were founded in Wisborough Green by the 1920s.

Wisborough Green Girl Guides camping in 1950. From left to right, back row: Voilet Dack, Hazel Williams, Daphne Clark, Vera Ford, Peggy Williams, Jane Eldridge, Josie Wakeford, Kathleen Hook. Front row: Joan Hook, Ada Harvey, Myrtle Willaims, Jenny Bagley.

A production of *Little Women* in 1942. From left to right, back row: -?-, Matti Owen/Kingston, Ruth West, Dorothy Newland, -?- , -?- , -?- . Front row: Audrey Radbourne, Joan Poat, Evelyn Foster, -?- , Helen Evershed. This group was a forerunner of the Billingshurst Dramatic Society, and was made up of all women players because most of the men were away at the war.

Billingshurst Dramatic Society production of *Lloyd George Knew My Father* at the Women's Hall. Left to right: John Humphreys, Ann Lawrence, Tony Smith, Angela Hughes, David Whelan, Sarah Haslem, Nevin Davis. Patrick Girth designed the stage set. He also designed the impressive Wisborough Green Tapestry, which is displayed in St Peter *Ad Vincula*.

Billingshurst Bonfire Society Fancy Dress, 1954. From left to right: Dennis Adams, Bill Burchell, -?- , Jimmy Wyatt.

Bill Phillips, as *Old Bill*, the First World War cartoon character who was created by Bruce Bairnsfather and first appeared in *The Bystander* in 1915.

Issued Fortnightly.
Gratis.

BONFIRE CELEBRATIONS.

The Fancy Dress Torchlight Procession and Bonfire was held with all its usual vim and excitement on Wednesday, November 4th. The Weather Clerk, fortunately, was kind to us, as he managed to sandwich a fine evening between two wet ones.

The judging for the Fancy Dress Competitions was held in the Village Hall before the Procession. The number of competitors was up to the average, in spite of a decided reduction in the entries in the classes for ladies. The following were the prize-winners, with character of costume given where possible. Owing to the new arrangements for distributing the prizes at the dance later in the week, there was not time to interview the successful competitors before they dispersed to join the procession.

Juveniles.—Character Costume: 1, Peter Voice (as Jim Mollison). 2, Margaret Andrews. 3, Cliff Griffin. Comic Costume: 1, Alan Dalmon. 2, Norah Skinner and Leslie Skinner (as the Bisto Kids).

Ladies.—Character Costume: 1, Mrs. Lloyd. 2, Mrs. Linfield.

Gentlemen.—Character Costume: 1, Mr. A. Symes. 2, Mr. R. Parsons. 3, Mr. W. Phillips (as Old Bill). Comic Costume: 1, Mr. G. King (as One of the Quads). 2, Mr. J. White (as a Monkey).

Most Original Costume.—1, Mr. F. Linfield (as a Coster). 2, Miss L. Andrews (as a Wax Doll). 3, Peter Bowring.

Best Home-made Costume.—Gentlemen: Mr. A. Watson. Juveniles: W. Skinner.

Mr. R. V. D. Cullen (Chairman of the Bonfire Society) presided. The Judges were Mrs. R. V. D. Cullen, Mrs. Cripps, Mrs. Pope, Mr. and Mrs. R. E. Norris, Rev. W. H. Sands, and Mr. W. Tribe. Messrs. A. E. Clark, E. Birchmore, and R. Crisp acted as Tellers.

Extract from *The Billingshurst News*, 14 November 1936. A report on the Bonfire celebration includes the results of the Fancy Dress Competition in which Bill Phillips came third.

Barkfold, which although situated in Kirdford parish is sometimes termed Barkfold, Wisborough Green! The grounds were used for the 1884 combined villages Flower Show. (Photograph by courtesy of West Sussex Library Service: Worthing Library.)

Receipts and Expenses of the Billingshurst, Wisborough Green, Loxwood, and Kirdford Cottage Garden Society, at their Annual Show at Barkfold, August 20th, 1884.

RECEIPTS FROM SUBSCRIPTIONS.

	£ s. d.		£ s. d.
Balance of 1883	1 19 5	Brought forward	22 10 11
R. Goff, Esq.	5 0 0	E. Braby, Esq.	0 10 0
Capt. and Mrs. Barwell	5 0 0	H. Tupper, Esq.	0 10 0
Rev. W. H. and Mrs. Barlee	2 2 6	Mrs. Shaw	0 10 0
W. Peachey, Esq., and Mrs. Peachey	1 11 0	F. Hayllar, Esq.	0 10 0
Rev. W. A. Bartlett	1 1 0	Rev. T. W. Fitch	0 10 0
Rev. G. Taylor	1 1 0	W. H. Hubert	0 10 0
H. Puttock, Esq.	1 1 0	Mrs. Francis	0 2 6
Mrs. Fynes Clinton	1 0 0	Mr. Sprinks	0 2 6
Mrs. J. Ireland	1 0 0	Mr. G. Hammond	0 2 6
H. Ireland, Esq.	0 15 0	Mr. E. Vickress	0 2 6
Lady Barttelot	0 10 0	Mr. J. S. Clark	0 2 6
Mrs. Schroeton	0 10 0	Mr. H. Jupp	0 2 6
		Mr. Jas. King	0 2 0
		Mr. Thos. Baker	0 2 6
Carried forward	£22 10 11		£26 15 5

RECEIPTS.

	£ s. d.
Total Subscriptions	26 15 5
Gate Money	4 12 11
Tea Tent	3 3 6
Cocoanut Game	1 7 6
Lawn Tennis	0 13 6
Exhibitors' Fees	1 1 5
	£37 14 3

EXPENSES.

	£ s. d.
Prizes	20 15 6
Band	6 6 0
Hire of Tents	5 17 0
Gatekeepers	0 5 0
Police	0 6 0
Stemp's Wagon to Billingshurst twice with Mr. Moore's plants	0 10 0
Dinner to 3 Judges and Mr. Moore's 2 men	0 10 0
Cake and Buns	0 19 7
Cocoanuts	0 10 0
Hire and breakage of Cups and Saucers	0 5 0
Bread	0 2 0
Mrs. G. Hillier, helping in Tea Tent	0 2 0
Printing (say)	2 0 0
	£38 8 1
Receipts	37 14 3
	£0 13 10

Billingshurst, Wisborough Green, Loxwood and Kirdford held a combined Flower Show for a number of years. These fell into abeyance sometime after 1887. Billingshurst revived its own show in 1903 and except for some of the war years it has been held ever since.

Matti Kingston, who is currently the president of the Billingshurst Horticultural Society, and her daughter Susan with their flower arrangements in 1969. This was the last time the Flower Show was held in a marquee in the recreation ground in Lower Station Road, but the Wisborough Green Flower Show still takes place in one.

Winners at the Wisborough Green Flower Show in 1966. Left to right: Frank Favell, secretary, Bill Mann and chairman George Goodchild who are showing their exhibits to Mr James, who sold the onion seeds to Mr Mann who then passed onions sets on to his friends. Mr James was the proprietor of the Handy Shop now 'gone from the Green'.

Tony Puttick with the cup he won in 1953 and 1954 for running fastest round the Green on Flower Show Day. His brother also won the race. The race continues to take place, but another cup has replaced the original one. The photograph was taken in the garden of 'Sunrise', his parent's home.

Wisborough Green football team 1956-7. From left to right, back row: William Goodchild, Pat Beer, Ernie Williams, Tony Puttick, John Goodchild, Percy Luxford. Front row: Len Sheppard, Laurie Cheesman, Jack Stocker, Denis Cooper, John Mann, Joe Cooper.

A victorious football team in the Recreation Ground in Lower Station Road, Billingshurst. From left to right, back row: Arthur Everson, Ken Pavey, Peter Long, Tony Radbourne, Jim Wyatt, John Church, Bill Phillips, Tom Topper, George Hollebone. Front row: Robin Stepney, Danny Cherriman, Harry Smith, Derek Adams, Eric Overington.

Billingshurst football team in the 1950s. From left to right, back row: Freddie Wells, Danny Cherriman, Harold Skinner, Ron Skinner, Herbie Parsons, Don Everson, Wally Redman. Front row: Paul Neuman, Harold Woods, Dennis Clark, Ken Pavey and Lionel Redman.

Billingshurst stool ball team. From left to right, front row: Myrtle Wells, -?- , Mrs Smith, Connie Richardson, -?- . Middle row: -?- , Joan Gray, Kath Denman, -?-, Marjorie Lugg. Back row: Mrs Claydon and Bet Collins.

Billingshurst School stool ball team in the 1930s. Miss Webb who was a teacher at the school for many years is on the left and the headmaster Mr Jeavons is on the right.

Wisborough Green stool ball team, in the 1950s. From left to right, back row: The scorer Mrs Luxford, Barbara Terry, Rose Mann, Sylvia Sherwood, Barbara Hammond, Josie Wakeford, Gladys Puttick and the umpire Mrs Farhall. Front row: Joan Luxford, Hazel Williams, Sylvia Farnfield, Eileen Bourne, -?- . (Photograph by George Garland, West Sussex Record Office copyright.)

Wisborough Green School sports team, c.1951. From left to right, back row: Tony Puttick, Terry Stemp, George Reeves, Ian Champion, J. De Mutt (?), Robin Eggledon, Romac Fillepa, Rodney Watson. Middle row: Stan Morgan, Brian Alder, Michael Gent, Tony Balloto (?), Jean Quickenden, Peggy Hunt, Angela Hook, -?- , Winnie Watson, Ann Quickenden. Front row: Joe Cooper, Mary Matthews, Eileen Bourne, Jenny Bagley, Colin Bagley.

117

Women's cricket team in 1925, at the Billingshurst Cricket Ground in Upper Station Road. The team was captained by Daisy Wadey of Newbridge Farm.

An early cricket photograph at Billingshurst. Freddie Wells is on the left of the middle row; he is the only person who can be accurately identified. He had many interests and was often photographed taking part in village events when younger and seen with a collecting box when older. The cricketer in the front row on the right appears in several other early cricket photographs.

A strong Wisborough Green cricket team, c.1960, although some of the players came from Billingshurst! From left to right, back row: Ian Sheppard, Fred Lee, Brian Cox, Tony Puttick, Sid Green, Doug Woods, Peter Vallis, Bill Puttick. Front row: Laurie Cheesman, Joe Pavey, Maurice Welford, John Mann, Nawab of Pataudi (Tiger) who later played for Sussex and captained India.

Peter Haigh's Eleven versus Wisborough Green, which was an Annual Charity Match. In September 1964 the celebrities, besides Peter Haigh, included Harry Secombe, Jill Adams (Mrs Haigh), Sir Leary Constantine and Bernard Cribbings. The president of Wisborough Green Club Felix Crawford, the son of the former headmaster of Wisborough Green School, is seen dressed in a collar and tie at the back. Pat Harrison, who must have been one of the youngest players, is in front of him.

Joseph Luxford on his tennis court situated on part of the allotment site by the bowling alley. Joe Luxford found time to play tennis and organize tennis tournaments despite owning a shop, running a Carrier business and playing a full part in village affairs; he was one of the original members of the Billingshurst Parish Council.

Winning tennis players in Billingshurst just before the Second World War. From left to right, front row: Nancy Holden, who later married Fred Allfrey, Revd Street, 'Girly' Verrall/Eve Brooks. Back row includes Fred Allfrey, who was killed in the RAF during the war, George Truelove, Sidney Matthews, Ronald Knight of Wisborough Green, Ernie Howell.

Five
The Two World Wars

Wisborough Green War Memorial in the 1960s. It bears the names of twenty-one men of the village who died during the First World War and ten who died during the Second World War. The memorial was paid for by public subscription and unveiled by Lord Leconfield in 1921. Remembered on the back of the memorial are the Canadian troops who never returned after the Dieppe raids in 1942 and who were previously stationed at Hawkhurst Court. The oak door to the church tower was presented by the Home Guard to commemorate the many fallen Canadians. During the First World War, the vicar of Wisborough Green the Revd Mainprice and his wife 'suffered the grievous loss of two gallant sons' who were in the Navy. There is a separate brass memorial to them inside the chancel arch. There is also a beautifully decorated brass plaque which remembers all the fallen of the Great War. Besides Ernest and Bernard Mainprice there are four other pairs of men with the same surname on the War Memorial. Two sons of Lt.-Col. Helme died in the conflict. Their home had been Lee Place, formerly in Pulborough parish; the property is now in Billinghurst parish but was always linked with Wisborough Green.

Billingshurst church tower and War Memorial. Fifty-five men of Billingshurst are remembered on the Billingshurst memorial from the First World War and twelve from the Second World War. In Billingshurst most of the men served in the Army during the First World War, and in the Army and Royal Air Force in the Second World War. From Wisborough Green a higher proportion served at sea in both World Wars. The vicars of Billingshurst and nearby Rudgwick both lost sons in the First World War.

Private John Ezra Bryant Beacher, known as Jack and seen on the far right of the back row. He was in the 13th Battalion, Royal Sussex Regiment, and was killed on 21 June 1916 aged twenty-one. He is buried in France. Jack Beacher is remembered on both the Billingshurst and Rudgwick War Memorials. His Uncle Edward was also in the same Section and is in the middle of the back row. He survived the conflict. Some members of their family still live in Billingshurst.

Henry and Jean Botting on their wedding day, pictured outside the Women's Hall in 1941. Henry's parents are on either side of the bride and bridegroom. Henry was granted compassionate leave to celebrate their marriage because he was on active service at the time. Henry served in the Royal Air Force Regiment from 1942 and went to France on D-Day with the 2809 Squadron. Jean came from Scotland and was employed at Gibbons Mill and Ingfield Manor. After her marriage she worked for two years on the land at Okehurst. Since the end of the war the couple have made their home in Billingshurst.

Francis William Goodchild, who was a Petty Officer serving on HMS *Pluckridge* when he was killed in 1943, aged thirty-two. He was a married man, the eldest son of William and Mary Goodchild, and called Sonny by his family. He is remembered on the Wisborough Green Memorial and on the Portsmouth Naval Memorial, because he has no known grave.

Arthur Mann of Wisborough Green, while he was a Private in the Royal Sussex Regiment. Arthur was wounded in the knee at the battle of the Somme. The result of the war injury had grave repercussions during his old age. He developed arthritis and had a stiff knee, then he had a stroke affecting the other side of his body and consequently spent the last three years of his life bedridden.

The three Mann brothers and their mother outside Chapel House sometime during the Second World War. From left to right: Wally Mann who was in the Army, Arthur Mann pictured above, in front, Emily, who was brought up as a Cokeler, Ernest Mann, who was a Chief Petty Officer on the *Ark Royal*.

Billingshurst veterans of the First World War returning to Flanders in the 1920s. They include Walter Goodhall, Henry Penfold, Ernie Scutt, George King, Bernard Baker the shopkeeper, Jimmy Puttock, George Wicks, and Bill Wicks.

Programme of Concert.
Arranged by ROBERT J. ABRAHAM.

Mrs. W. SHEPHERD
 PIANOFORTE SELECTION   "Pot Pourri"

Mr. HARRY TAYLOR
 HUMOROUS SONGS   "My Wife's first Husband"
          "All about Love"
          "The Ideal Home"

Mr. WILL BARDEN
 (1.) VENTRILOQUIAL SKETCH
 (2.) MIMICRY

Mr. W. A. LAUDER
 SONGS   " 'Hats off' to the Stoker"
      "The Trumpeter"
      "Shipmates of Mine"

Mr. W. SHEPHERD
 HUMOROUS SONGS   "The Boarding House"
         "Man," by one who 'loathes' him.

Mr. J. BURDFIELD
 SONGS   "Jack's the Boy"
      "The Deserter"

Mr. RUNNICLES
 HUMOROUS SONGS   "Gallery and Boxes"
         "Shurr-up"

Mr. C. JOYES
 SONGS   "As your Hair grows Whiter"
      " 'Allo, my Baby"

Mr. R. WOOD
 SONGS   Selected.

At the Piano, Mrs. W. SHEPHERD.

— GOD SAVE THE KING. —

Re-union Supper & Social Evening
— FOR —

SERVICE & EX-SERVICE MEN

of Billingshurst.

Wednesday, 13th August, 1919,
— AT —
S. Mary's Hall, Billingshurst.

Chairman: REV. R. O. JOHNS.

Committee:
Messrs. J. A. Craft (*Chairman*), A. E. Graham,
O. Pennicard, G. Argent, R. Wadey, W. Pavey,
C. Harrison, A. Lusted, C. M. Joyes, F. Blake,
W. Wicks, F. Harris, A. A. Thomas, W. Tribe,
R. J. Abraham.

Wm. C. Pilcher, *Hon. Sec. & Treasurer.*

Reunion Programme.

A German Prisoner of War hanging out his washing at the camp in Marringdean Road in 1945. (Courtesy of *Soldier* magazine of the British Army.)

The wedding of Radolt Hugley and Mabel Newton at Gore farm in 1948. Mabel, who came from Mansfield, was a Landgirl and had digs at Gore Farm and was married from there. Radolt had been a Prisoner of War at the camp in Marringdean Road. Later he lived in a caravan at Todhurst with his friend Franz Trudnovski, where he met Mabel. After the war, Radolt worked at Newbridge Farm. On the right, is the best man Franz Trudnovski, Radolt, Gordon Lugg, Mabel, Ada Lugg and in front Michael and Roger Lugg. Radolt is now over ninety and lives at Broomers Hill.

Iris Woods and Joyce, two Landgirls who worked for the Sherlock family at Renvyle.

The Luggs Landgirls threshing gang in 1945. Left to right: Iris Clark who came from Southwick and stayed in Billingshurst to marry Ernie Ayre of Lordings, Babs from Devon, Mabel, whose wedding photograph is shown previously and Joan who came from Nottingham.

Officers of the Home Guard, Red Cross and WVS. The Billingshurst people recognized are: Dr Hope-Gill, Mr Butler, Ernie Ayre, Rudolf Fielding, Mrs Rogerson, Miss Puttock, Col. Kerr, Mrs Norris.

The artist Harold Roberts came to England with the Canadian Expeditionary Force during the First World War. During the Second World War he served with the Royal Sussex Regiment. He was a permanent Staff Instructor with the rank of Regimental Sergeant Major working with the Home Guard.